# REFRESHING
## YOUR SOUL

Caring for Your Inner Life

# REFRESHING YOUR SOUL

## Caring for Your Inner Life

PRESENTED BY

## JILL BRISCOE

COMPILED BY
## SHELLY ESSER

*Just Between Us*, Brookfield, Wisconsin 53045

REFRESHING YOUR SOUL

This book is part of a series on relevant topics from *Just Between Us* Magazine. For more information about *Just Between Us*, please turn to the back of this book.

The Team: Suzan Braun, Kate Habrel, Jeanette Kay, Nancy Krull, Debbie Leech, Mary Perso

Cover & Layout Design: Sophie Beck

# just between us

1 **Escaping to God's Arms** by Jane Rubietta
Tools and tips for planning a personal spiritual retreat with God........ 9

2 **Exchanging Calm for Chaotic** by Nancy Slack
One woman's experience of release and renewal while on a spiritual
retreat.................................................................................. 13

3 **RX: Soul Medicine** by Shelly Esser
Laughter can lift your soul in life's most difficult times ...................... 16

4 **Is Solitude Possible in a Noisy World?** by Shelly Esser
How to become comfortable with solitude and use it to refresh your
soul...................................................................................... 20

5 **Running Out of Prayers** by Jill Briscoe
Discover how you can jump-start your prayer life when you feel like
you're running out of prayers and praying is just too hard.................. 23

6 **How to Hear God's Voice Above the Clamor** by Stacey Padrick-Thompson
How to incorporate contemplative prayer into your everyday life........ 28

7 **20 Ways to Wake Up Your Quiet Time** by Pam Farrel
Creative, thoughtful ways for energizing your quiet time with God..... 32

8 **Rest for the Weary** by Denele Ivins
A missionary shares the importance of getting away from it all to renew
your spirit – especially when you don't think you can afford the time... 37

9 **Soul Care** by Linda Kline
Questions to ask yourself when assessing the state of your soul in the
whirlwind of your busy life................................................... 41

10 **Food for the Soul** by Jean Fleming
The many benefits of spending regular alone time with God.............. 44

# REFRESHING
## YOUR SOUL

We live in a non-stop, chaotic world. Caring for our families, ministering to friends, and everyday responsibilities often leave us tired and depleted–and with no time left for ourselves and God. Yet our souls desperately need time with God–for the spiritual renewal and replenishment only He can bring. In these 10 chapters, you'll learn why personal spiritual care is so necessary. You'll read personal experiences of "soul care," from retreats and sabbaticals to creative ideas you can do at home. And you'll see how easy it is to create some personal "soul time" with God every day.

# 1

# Escaping to God's Arms

## Tools and tips for planning a personal spiritual retreat with God.

### by Jane Rubietta

The walls of winter closed in on me, squeezing the breath from my soul and the light from my heart. Any love that might have filtered down at Christmas had long since disappeared into the tundra. I scraped–and scraped–my way through the icy grip of a frozen holiday season and trudged into January, but the internal bleakness turned dark as night. From the deep caverns one thought surfaced: Run away. And then, run to God for a personal retreat.

In God's fun timing, our daughter left me the keys to her apartment in Chicago, and I hopped a train through slush and sludge. As my daily world receded, my perspective changed. I could begin to hear my heart's cry, examine my longings, and turn toward God's arms again.

## A PERSONAL RETREAT: WHAT IT IS – AND IS NOT

A personal retreat is an escape into the calm, loving embrace of God. It is a flight from the front lines of battle to the medic station, where we leave the gun-slinging to someone else – and holster our weapons for a time. A personal retreat is a safe place where we can distance ourselves from all our activities, responsibilities, and relationships, and in that detachment find God's perspective.

In a personal retreat, whether a cozy afternoon in the living room, a sit-in on a park bench, or an overnight getaway, we separate from the situations, roles, and behaviour that form or reinforce our self-esteem – or lack of self-esteem. The personal retreat is both antithesis and antidote to the constant clamoring noise of our inner and outer world. In the solitude and stillness of retreat, we no longer need to earn our keep or make people happy. Nothing matters in this safe place except the state of our own body and soul.

The point of retreat is not to check off a bunch of to-dos. It is not to set new goals, although I read one esteemed scholar recommending just that. It is not to work on overdue tasks or catch up on correspondence or run errands.

The point of retreat is to meet with God. To love God, to be loved by God, to rest in that love, and to be restored to love well in our daily lives. The Psalmist says, in Ps. 119:114 (MSG), "You're my place of quiet retreat; I wait for your Word to renew me." In personal retreat, our focus shifts away from the undones, the poorly dones, already dones, wish-I-hadn't-dones. On retreat, we make eye contact with Jesus once again. Without that critical eye contact, "fixing our eyes on Jesus," we cannot continue to "run the race with endurance" (Heb. 12:1-2, NASB).

In her book, *A Generous Presence*, Rochelle Melander writes, "And this rest – this letting go of being in charge and really resting can fill us up again... Our mind, body, and spirit need time off to strengthen itself for the next shift of working as well. Runners who do not take the time out for their body to adapt, run the risk of injury. Those of us who do not let our minds and spirits rest risk the injury of our souls. Truly, rest is healing."

## JESUS ON RETREAT

During our first pastorate, I watched with longing and, honestly, a great deal of envy as my husband packed the orange college backpack for his regular personal retreat. I wanted someone to magically deliver me, in the throes of parenting, to show up at my door offering child care and housekeeping while I whistled off toward the horizon.

After several morose months, I recognized the pattern Jesus established. In the midst of heavy ministry, inquisitions from detractors, enraged synagogue leaders, and brilliant never-seen-before miracles, He took His need to connect deeply with God all the more seriously: "Jesus often withdrew to lonely places and prayed" (Luke 5:16).

Retreat seemed to help Jesus hear God's directives, as well: "One of those days Jesus went out to a mountainside to pray, and spent the night praying to God. When morning came, he called his disciples to him and chose twelve of them" (Luke 6:12-13).

After John the Baptist's beheading by Herod, the Scriptures say, "When Jesus heard what had happened, he withdrew by boat privately to a solitary place" (Matt. 14:13). It would appear that Christ needed separation in order to grieve, and focus on God's purpose and calling.

Jesus also gave permission: "Come with me by yourselves to a quiet place and get some rest" (Mark 6:31). While I was waiting for human beings to set things in motion, Jesus had already done so, and was waiting for me to take those first steps into a deeper relationship.

Jesus balanced work and withdrawal, solitude and service, engagement and disengagement. Part of the secret to His focus, His power,

His wisdom, comes from intense time with His Father. And if He needed that time away, alone with God, how much more do we?

## WHERE-TOS

Whether you're hoping for an afternoon of solitude, an overnight, or a longer stretch of time, consider where you best hear God. Roughing it in a slim bunk in a cold cabin may render you deaf! My destination varies depending on my needs. If physical rest is your primary spiritual need, the room may be more important than the grounds around it. Or maybe a church pew would be perfect. During one season, my primary question was, "Do you have a bathtub?"

Maybe you simply need a blanket, rations, and a lawn chair. Ask yourself, "What does my soul long for? My body? My creative self? Where might I best hear God?" Maybe your answer is, "In nature." What about a friend with a cabin you could borrow, or a colleague's sun room, or someone's finished basement? Consider state parks, monasteries, convents, and retreat houses–as long as you are alone, and don't have to be hospitable. You can do that with the rest of your life; this time is for your soul, alone.

Wherever you retreat, inquire about amenities. Do you need basics like coffee or bedding? And don't forget to ask about daily bread.

Think through your comfort needs, unless you crave a Desert Fathers' and Mothers' type experience. Which may be exactly the paring down you seek to escape all the strictures and structures of life and work and get down to who you really are, ready to really listen.

## TOOLS FOR RETREAT

People often ask, "What would I do alone for all that time?" "Nothing" is not a comforting response for people who do, do, do. Many spiritual disciplines apply to the personal retreat. Silence, worship, thoughtful reading of Scripture, meditation, journaling. Maybe you'll ask God to highlight a text for you to hold fast during your time, inviting the Holy Spirit to bring the Word home to your heart and life.

Ask, "What do I need from God?" Is it rest? Or love? Or direction, or simply refilling, or a quickening in your soul through Scripture? Your answer helps determine what will nurture your soul and engage with God.

I bring a hymnal, a journal, a meaty reading from a classic writer, my Bible. I tend to overload my book bag, and ultimately overlook the main point of retreat. This is no place to attempt to over-achieve.

Maybe your highest goal for retreat is to sleep without an alarm. Didn't Jesus say, "Come to me, all who are weary and heavy-laden, and

I will give you rest" (Matt. 11:28, NASB)?

## RE-ENTRY

As the time draws near to return, I start leaving a timeless place and measuring: only 24 more hours. Twelve. Six. One. I dread withdrawing from this "lonely place." When I begin to return, I feel a little like the shuttle on "Apollo 13," with a re-entry slot as thick as an envelope. The chances of successfully slipping through that niche are smaller than the chance of my winning a triathlon (which is zero, if you're interested). Emerging from solitude may be a culture shock, re-engaging in relationships like trying to hug people while wearing a straitjacket or a space suit.

Toward the end of the retreat, I turn my prayer focus toward my loved ones and my profession. I consciously lower my expectations of my family, the state of home, laundry, or refrigerator. I ask God for an extra measure of love to pour out, and to hold my heart near to His so that I am more continually reminded of His presence, His joy, His delight in me. I try to cement what God has conveyed to me through the silence and solitude, where He challenged, loved, rebuked. What is the "takeaway," condensed to one sentence?

Ultimately, when we slip away to a quiet place, we can rest in God's love. And women who are loved, become loving. Which is just what our families and friends need.

# 2

# Exchanging Calm for Chaotic

**One woman's experience of release and renewal while on a spiritual retreat.**

### by Nancy Slack

I opened the back door of the monastery and walked down the hill. The grass slapped against my ankles, and the air smelled like rain. I sat on a dry rock next to the river and closed my eyes.

I needed this retreat. The past year had been awful. At home, my husband and I struggled with childlessness. I missed my mother, who had died the year before. At work, my department had been reorganized, and I'd worked so much I'd had little time to pray.

But here in the mountains of New Mexico, with morning air pressing like ice on my skin, I could forget the past year and reconnect with God.

I tried to listen, but the conflicts of the past year swarmed into my mind. Why had the department head dumped all of those extra meetings on me? Why didn't the principal help?

I opened my eyes and saw the river splashing white and cold at my feet. This was a beautiful place. I wanted to enjoy it, not irritably dredge up problems I'd sooner leave behind.

I stood up and brushed the dirt off my skirt. I'd try to pray again later.

That evening I sat on a hard plastic chair in the sanctuary and listened to the chanting of the Psalms. As the monks sat quietly in prayer, silence spread over the room like a mist. I closed my eyes.

But instead of prayer, I thought of a baby shower at work. We'd sat in a circle, passing around small ruffled outfits and tiny baby books with hard wooden covers. The woman sitting next to me at the shower had peered into my face. "And why don't you have any children?" she had said.

In the quiet of the monastery, I remembered her question. My eyes felt hot, and I blinked back tears. I shook my head.

"God, this is crazy," I thought. "Help me."

But the next day, the more I reached for peace, the more chaotic I felt. I sat next to a creek in the mountains, watching my husband fish – and saw a picture of my mother's face when she died. I walked on a mountain trail, passing clumps of wild iris – and wondered if I should quit my job.

I'd come to the retreat to get close to God. But my prayer life steered like a small boat swamped by emotions on all sides: grief, resentment, irritation, and rage.

"God," I thought, "what is wrong with me?"

That evening I walked along the bank of the river and watched the water churn over flat brown rocks. I sat under trees whose roots rippled the ground. I saw a creek seep past a dam of sticks until the water broke free and poured into the river.

After a while, something occurred to me. Sometimes chaos is normal.

I had spent the last few months with a rictus stretched across my face. I had not dealt with problems; I had ignored them.

And now these difficulties kept reappearing, especially when I prayed. Maybe God wanted me to quit pretending I was fine. Like a little kid with a splinter, I needed to sit still and let Him take care of me – even if I was uncomfortable in the process.

I remembered a verse I liked from the Psalms.

"Trust in him at all times, O people; pour out your hearts to him, for God is our refuge" (Ps. 62:8).

Over the next few days, I needed to systematically release every problem to God. He wanted me to pour out my heart to Him, allowing sorrow and anger and bitterness to surface. I could not handle such huge emotions on my own – but God could.

So I spent the next few days in places that shimmered with light and water, telling God all about the problems that had occurred in other places. I sat in the sanctuary and repented of resentments I'd fostered in the past year. I walked a path through the meadow and forgave people who had hurt me at work. I threw rocks in the river and told God the names of children I might never have.

I swam in emotions that had been submerged so long they threatened to overwhelm me. I found solace in another verse from the Psalms.

"When my spirit grows faint within me, it is you who know my way. In the path where I walk men have hidden a snare for me" (Ps. 142:3).

I wrote the verse on a note card and stuck it in my Bible.

Sometimes, it seemed, faith could be a strange experience. I wanted my prayer life to be happy and cheerful, not this chaotic emotional mess. But God wanted me to trust Him with it all. Over time, He would take care of everything. Over time, all would be well.

The morning light shone on stark hills of red dirt and green pinyon trees as we drove home from New Mexico. In a small town in West Texas, we pulled into a roadside café.

I walked into the early morning air conditioning and stopped, struck by the words on a poster on the wall. "Darrell," I called to my husband. "Darrell, look at this."

We read the poster together.

> Why are you surprised at the
> CHAOS
> Inside you
> When you have asked for
> JESUS
> To renew you
> To remodel you
> To change everything about you?

I wrote the words on a napkin. The coincidence of this word on a café wall – this word that had appeared over and over in my journal that week – seemed like no accident. For a moment, in a café in West Texas, I could see that the chaos in my life was part of a larger pattern, one that was being gently controlled and guided the whole time.

# 3

# Rx:Soul Medicine

**Laughter can lift your soul in life's most difficult times.**

### by Shelly Esser

Not long ago my family was sitting around the dinner table after finishing a meal just lingering in the joy of each other's company. I don't even remember what we were talking about, but before I knew it we were all erupting in laughter—the deep belly, tears running down your cheeks kind, and I remember thinking it felt so good to laugh like that. In fact, I couldn't remember the last time I had laughed that hard. In those precious moments something happened to my soul. I was no longer carrying around the heaviness of the difficult days and circumstances which had crushed my spirit for months, but instead felt a sense of release as I allowed myself to have a good laugh. I felt a surge of strength come into my spirit that I hadn't felt for a long time and so desperately needed. Proverbs 17:22 says in the New Living Translation, "A cheerful heart is good medicine, but a broken spirit saps a person's strength." I think that's what happened at the table that night, suddenly my sapped strength was being re-energized by laughter–and it was good medicine to my soul.

There are over 50 references about laughter in the Bible. And in the verse in Proverbs, it says that laughter holds as much healing power as medicine. In fact, research has confirmed this and shown laughter to be therapeutic. There are health centers across the country treating patients suffering from conditions like depression, stress, and diabetes with laughter therapy. Now medical science agrees with what the Bible has said about the benefits of laughter. According to a study conducted by the University of Maryland, laughter is a powerful remedy for stress, pain, and conflict. Nothing works faster or more dependably to bring your mind and body back into balance after a good laugh. Laughter lightens your burdens, inspires hope, connects you to others, and keeps you more focused on the positive. Furthermore, it relaxes the whole body relieving physical tension and stress, leaving your muscles relaxed for up to 45 minutes later. It boosts the immune system, triggers the release of endorphins, the body's natural feel-good chemicals promoting an overall sense of well-being, and can even temporarily relieve pain. And laughter protects the heart. Wow, God knew what He was doing when He gave us the prescription of laughter.

Perhaps, there is no greater time in our lives for the soul medicine of laughter or a "cheerful heart" than when we're going through life's most difficult times. If you think about it, those times are too often characterized by just the opposite, depleting us of all our strength making it hard to persevere. Once our strength disappears, our spirits so easily become crushed. But God has a remedy for us. In the middle of our hardships, God can come in and heal our souls through the simple medicine of laughter or humor. Not that the hardship is funny in any way; it isn't! But we are given some relief through the laughter itself—something our soul desperately needs if we're to live uncrushed in spirit. Nehemiah 8:10 further confirms this: "The joy of the Lord is your strength." In the Greek, joy means "cheerfulness." And a cheerful heart is a continual medicine strengthening us both inwardly and outwardly.

A month ago, I was struck by the comments of one of our missionaries whose husband was dying of cancer. While he was in hospice care she wrote, "Although Dave is having increasing pain these days and needs help getting to the bed and to the couch and back again, he still has his sense of humor and gets me laughing at different times during the day." Laughing during cancer? Yes, laughter was God's way of increasing their strength in the midst of the impossible. This couple was experiencing the medicine for their souls that comes in the relief of laughter. Somehow laughter interspersed with the days and weeks of deep grief and sadness can make the unbearable bearable. Life can get so heavy and laden with burdens, but laughter gives us a break so that we can carry on in the midst of them. It doesn't take the pain away, but it does provide a much-needed emotional break. Again, Proverbs reminds us that laughter is good medicine for our beaten down souls. That's what the missionary wife was saying. It was her husband's humor that was giving them relief—strength for the next moment. There will still be tears, but there can also be joy from funny, light-hearted moments.

I recently read an online article about Bob Carey whose wife, Linda, is battling breast cancer, which is not incurable. Bob is a middle-aged photographer with a bit of a belly taking completely ridiculous photos of himself in various locations in a pink tutu all to hear his wife laugh. Bob has braved the snow in his pink tutu. He even traveled to Italy—

in his pink tutu! He said, "When Linda would go in for treatment, she would take the images on her phone and the women would look at them and it would make them laugh and make the time pass." (Now through the Tutu Project, which was started by the Careys for women battling breast cancer, the photos are available in a calendar.) The Careys' foundation strives to bring laughter to a community that has endured far too much. "Oddly enough," Bob said, "Linda's cancer has taught us that life is good, dealing with it can be hard, and sometimes the very best thing—no, the only thing—we can do to face another day is to laugh at ourselves, and share a laugh with others." Laughter gives us a sense of comfort that often provides us with the encouragement we need to face what is before us with renewed strength.

God created laughter and humor because He knew that we would need the soul medicine it provides in this fallen world. So how do we take this soul medicine and make it part of our daily spiritual health regimen?

**1. Find your funny bone and tickle it.** One of the nightly rituals I started during some really hard years was to watch the back-to-back reruns of *Frasier* before bed. They made me laugh so hard, and for an hour every night my weary soul was strengthened. Those minutes of laughter lightened the load of my heart and gave me a break. Find what tickles your funny bone and make it a regular habit to build time for laughter into your life.

**2. Surround yourself with people who live life joyfully.** Have friends in your circle who know how to have fun and have a good sense of humor and can make you laugh—people who can find humor in the day-to-day events. Laughter is contagious. I had the blessing of growing up in a home with a mother who had a great sense of humor and fun. It has been a therapeutic blessing throughout my life to spend time with her and to be reminded to laugh and enjoy life even in hard times. Laughter has a way of bonding us together and reminding us that we're all in this together, so let's have some fun along the way.

**3. Ask God to help you find something to laugh about even when it seems like there's nothing to laugh about.** Look for the funny, lighthearted things in life. There are a lot of joyful moments in our lives when we train ourselves to look for them. Even when there has been nothing to laugh about in my circumstances, God has helped me to find the humor in some small thing.

**4. Count your blessings.** As you begin to intentionally count your blessings, you will find your heart becoming more merry or cheerful instead of discouraged. We can find something to be thankful for even in the difficult times. As we practice thanking God, we begin to see our blessings more clearly. And there is something wonderful about a grateful spirit; it does wonders for our heart and outlook in general.

**5. Develop a sense of humor.** So often we take ourselves too seriously. Certainly there are those times in life that are not occasions for laughter, but most of life is ordinary living and we can choose whether to find laughter and joy or not. It can often begin by learning to laugh at ourselves and looking for the funny around us.

James Martin said, "Joy, humor, and laughter should be part of everyone's spiritual life. They are gifts from God." Hand-in-hand, faith and laughter is the best medicine for your soul. From the beginning, God knew how important laughter would be in our lives long before the medical world ever discovered the incredible benefits to our physical and mental health. It's an important practice to develop if we're going to survive in this broken world. So look for things to laugh about. Try focusing on the blessings rather than only on the difficulties in your life. Find ways to tickle your funny bone. Use the gift that God has given and laugh! It's good medicine for your soul.

# 4

# Is Solitude Possible in a Noisy World?

**How to become comfortable with solitude and use it to refresh your soul.**

### by Shelly Esser

A college friend who is a missionary in a Third World country was recently over for dinner while he was here for a mission festival. I was surprised when he mentioned the need for solitude in his life. I had just been thinking about resurrecting solitude – which is the temporary state of being alone for spiritual purposes – in my own life, and that it just might be an anecdote to the daily stresses we all experience.

Before I made some necessary changes, I started observing my life. I became increasingly aware of how much noise filled my life and altered my inner peace. In the morning I turned on the TV to hear the news and weather; in the car driving to work I played Christian CDs; once I got to work, I turned on the computer and was immersed in busyness and interaction with others; on the way home from work I listened to more music. Well, you get the picture. With a flip of the switch, my life was being inundated with everything but solitude. And we wonder why we're so stressed.

Upon my discovery, I began intentionally not flipping on a switch and instead just learning to be comfortable without the noise. That was really hard at first and is a continual challenge, because I have developed such a *noise* habit. I think many of us are afraid of quiet. We don't know what to do with it. We feel guilty and unproductive. Often, however, it is the very noise that contributes to our stressful lives. Without building pauses for solitude into our lives, we become enslaved to a frenetically-paced and stressful lifestyle. But, by turning off the noise switches, a funny thing began to happen. I started to hear God's whispers again and experience a settling peace.

There is something transforming about silence and solitude. There are times we need to hear the voice of God and what it is He wants us to spend our time on. Solitude is a place for us to sift through feelings and attitudes, to refresh our weary souls, and to just adore and behold God. Our spirits actually crave solitude and silence, but our culture conditions us for just the opposite – to be comfortable with crowds and noise. In her book, *Living the Christ-centered Life Between Walden and the Whirlwind*, author Jean Fleming says, "We live in a noisy, busy world. Silence and solitude are not twentieth-century words. They fit the era of Victorian lace, high-button shoes, and kerosene lamps better than our age of television, video arcades, and joggers wired with earphones. We have become a people with an aversion to quiet and uneasiness with being alone."

Those people that I know who have the deepest walks with God are those who have been often and long *alone* with Him. They have come to practice the discipline of solitude in their lives regularly. For most of us, this will be a constant battle. The enemy is well aware of the stakes involved in a lifestyle that incorporates solitude. Martyred missionary Jim Elliot said, "I think the devil has made it his business to monopolize on three elements: noise, hurry, crowds…Satan is quite aware of the power of silence." Unless we plan for times of solitude – wherever they may be found – our lives will become one big ineffective cycle of stress and spiritual shallowness.

Solitude helps us become physically and spiritually refreshed. Jesus told His disciples to "Come with me by yourselves to a quiet place and get some rest" (Mark 6:31). They needed to be refreshed and Jesus knew that solitude was the remedy.

Scripture uses many examples of people demonstrating the need for solitude. Jesus in Matthew 14:23 "…went up on a mountainside by himself to pray." In Mark 1:35 Jesus "Very early in the morning, while it was still dark, …got up, left the house and went off to a solitary place, where he prayed." Habakkuk 2:20 says, "But the LORD is in his holy temple; let all the earth be silent before him." Zephaniah 1:7 says, "Be silent before the Sovereign LORD…" In Psalm 62 David says in verses 1-2, "My soul waits in silence for God only…" (NASB).

So how do you build solitude into a noisy life? By capturing the moments. Solitude may last only a few minutes or it can go on for days in a retreat setting. Instead of flipping on the radio or the TV, spend those moments in solitude. I've found the car – without passengers – to be one of the greatest opportunities to grab a few uninterrupted minutes of solitude. Other places might be while you're waiting for kids, or in the shower (my favorite place). Try to find those times in your routine to silence your life and commune with God and watch how He empowers your busiest days and diffuses your stress.

Find creative places for solitude. They can be in your workplace, your home, your ministry setting, outdoors in God's creation, or on short or long retreats. I love the story of Susannah Wesley, the mother of John and Charles, and 15 other children! It was said that when her children noticed her in the parlour with her huge hoop skirt petticoats pulled up over her head that she was not to be disturbed because she was praying – capturing a few minutes of alone time with God!

How often are you alone so you can really hear God's voice? Think about that for a minute. The busier, more hectic your life is, the more you need to capture those moments of silence and solitude. Turn off the noise in your life and reach for solitude instead – it will be the very practice that will restore your soul and reduce your stress.

# 5

# Running Out of Prayers

**Discover how you can jump-start your prayer life when you feel like you're running out of prayers and praying is just too hard.**

by Jill Briscoe

Have you ever run out of prayers? I'm sure you have. Was it after failure or success? We can understand our prayer life being affected when we are in trouble, but what about it being affected by achievement?

After Elijah ran to Jezreel, toward victory and acclamation, God vindicated him by fire. But suddenly Elijah turns and runs in the opposite direction.

When Ahab got home, he told Jezebel that Elijah had slaughtered the prophets of Baal. "So Jezebel sent this message to Elijah: 'May the gods also kill me if by this time tomorrow I have failed to take your life like those whom you killed'" (1 Kings 19:2).

Elijah was afraid and fled for his life. He went to Beersheba, and on alone into the desert. "He sat down under a solitary broom tree and prayed that he might die. 'I have had enough, LORD,' he said. 'Take my life, for I am no better than my ancestors'" (1 Kings 19:4, NLT).

Elijah runs away from Jezreel and into the jaws of defeat. He was just like us, human and afraid. Yes, he was afraid! (1 Kings 19:3).

This particular verse of Scripture is an amazing verse. I could imagine the Bible saying that Elijah was exhausted or angry or lonely, but not "Elijah was afraid"! Yet, that particular verse of Scripture encourages me to keep hoping, because I, too, am often afraid.

What do we do when we run out of faith and run into fear? Do we end up like Elijah, flat on our faces under the proverbial broom tree (v. 4)?

It has been my experience that when you run into fear you can run out of faith in a hurry. Fear paralyzes you. I have always been a fearful person. When I was a child, I feared I wouldn't ever grow up. When I did grow up, I feared I would never live long enough to get married. When I got married, I was frightened I would never have children.

When I had three, I worried that they would never get married and have children. And so on and so forth.

I am very familiar with the fear that chases faith away. It can all happen in a moment! It might feel final, as I'm sure it did to Elijah, but as we shall see, this fear would lead to a whole new dimension of ministry and experience in prayer.

## WHAT FEAR DOES TO FAITH

Stuart and I live in Wisconsin, where snow and ice are a big part of our lives during the long winter months. Sometimes we get a blizzard. You can be inching along, and all of a sudden you run into what is called a "whiteout." You literally go blind for a moment and become disoriented as the snow swirls around the windshield.

We can experience whiteouts in our faith life too. We could call these experiences "doubt outs." You see perfectly clear one moment, and the next you are blinded by the storm. Doubt is faith in distress, and it is very hard to pray when you are doubting God. The Bible says, "Anyone who wants to come to him must believe that there is a God and that he rewards those who sincerely seek him" (Heb. 11:6, NLT). Elijah was experiencing a mammoth "doubt out." He couldn't see God anymore, but he could see Jezebel. And she looked so much bigger than God.

It's funny what things people are afraid of, isn't it? Here is Elijah, who has taken on an entire nation, running away from a woman! But then, doubt and exhaustion do strange things to you. It's easy to lose perspective.

## WHAT GOD'S PRESENCE DOES FOR US

The first thing to do when you arrive under the broom tree is to quit everything. Elijah didn't pretend. He simply said, "God, I've had it!" Elijah was experiencing serious burnout. Be encouraged to be this honest when your turn comes. God wants us to say whatever we want to say.

If we are talking about intercession, we must believe that God is a rewarder of "those who sincerely seek him." When you're under the broom tree, your prayers are not intercessory prayers but rather prayers of desperation. Yet author Ole Hallesby encourages us to pray on, even when we are driving through a blizzard of unbelief! He says,

*Many have had most remarkable answers to prayer when they had no clear or definite assurance that they would be heard. It has seemed to them that God has given the most remarkable answers to prayer at times when they had no faith whatsoever!*

So keep talking to the Lord even if you are mad at Him or doubting His very existence. Jesus promised that a sparrow would never fall without the Father knowing it. Note, He never promised that a sparrow would not fall, but He did promise the sparrow would not fall without the Father's knowledge of it. God is never surprised by our visits to the broom tree.

So let's see what happened to the humbled prophet under his trauma tree.

## GOD DEALS WITH OUR DISAPPOINTMENT

I find that when I'm checking into the Broom Tree Inn, I lose my perspective of God. All I can think about is how disappointed God must be with me. I become convinced that He is telling me to get my act together and share the *Four Spiritual Laws* with Jezebel!

I have to remind myself that I can never surprise God. In fact, all that God expects from us is failure of one kind or another along our spiritual road. The good news is, He waits around the corner of our failure. He has a plan – a plan of renewal and refreshment – and He waits at the reception desk of Broom Tree Inn, ready and eager to check us in! What we need to do is cooperate. We should lie down and sleep again (1 Kings 19:5-7).

Whatever medicine God the Healer prescribes, we should take it. And we should rest long enough for the loving treatment to take effect. Elijah waited until he was strong enough to go on before he went on.

What brought you to this point? Was it a church that hurt you or a spouse that abandoned you? Maybe you are under the broom tree because of things you cannot change. Perhaps you are the victim of a cruel circumstance. Wrong choices that others made have had severe consequences for you. Perhaps, like Elijah, you are mostly disappointed with yourself. It is only a matter of time before you decide that God can do without you and so can everyone else!

I can remember getting into that state of mind only once. My husband was out of town and my father was sick. Things were not going well in the youth work I was responsible for, and then our daughter broke her arm. Stuart was in America making plans for us to immigrate and I was supposed to be wrapping up our work and packing up the house.

One day I couldn't ignore the gnawing pain in my stomach anymore, so I went to the doctor. He told me I was suffering from an ulcer, and he put me in the hospital. Suffering from a great imagination as well as a bleeding ulcer, I was quite sure that I was going to die and that this would be a lot better for all concerned. God would give Stuart an American wife who could do the job in the States a whole lot better than I could, and everyone would benefit.

As I think back to how the Lord lifted me out of my deep despond-ency, I realize that God may have allowed me to go through it so I could encourage others. Looking back I can see that my experience was not unlike Elijah's.

The first thing both of us received was physical help. If you are in this predicament, have yourself checked out. It isn't unspiritual to look after your body. People helped me practically, and I had to learn to let them. God brought Elijah breakfast; friends brought my family supper!

And then I found lots of help in the Word about God's great concern for me. "The journey is too great for you," I read over and over again. God was not mad at me for being in the state I was in; He was loving and caring and infinitely patient. Above all, I became convinced that God was not finished with me yet. Failure is never final.

God "touched" His servant Elijah at the lowest point of his life, and God touched me as well. I continued on my way, strengthened by the nourishment He provided through the Bible, Christian friends, and above all, prayer. God will find a way to touch you if you give Him a chance to minister grace to you.

## WHAT THE BROOM TREE EXPERIENCE GIVES TO US

The broom tree experiences in our lives introduce us to a new way of praying. It's not verbal praying but rather a total abandonment of ourselves in despair at God's feet. It is a wordless praying, a silent scream for help. Sometimes we cannot even shout at God. We are spent.

When you run out of prayers, God can still hear you! Even though no words are formed or spoken, God looks at you and reads the lan-guage of your longing. At that moment, you see, you are the prayer! So be content to just be a desperate prayer under your particular broom tree, and wait and see what happens!

You may wonder how long you will be there. You'll remain there as long as it takes for you to be strengthened. Try not to take on any-thing extra until things begin to be resolved. Once Elijah was off and running again, God went ahead of him, preparing his future. That is definitely what happened to me.

Stuart said that I had to stay put in England until I was well enough to face the immigration process, and I gradually regained my health and began to pack for the journey to the States. God went ahead of me every step of the way.

How will you know God has touched you and that it is time to move on? You will know if you sense God's love and acceptance. You will feel this sense of inner well-being far deeper than at the emotional level. The Holy Spirit does not come into our hearts to do His deepest work in the shallowest part of us. He works His healing grace at the mind level first. Once you hear Him saying something kind and sweet, believe it, get up from under your broom tree and go on to Horeb, the mountain of God.

If Elijah had not believed that "God was not finished with him yet," he would have died of a broken heart under the broom tree. If I had not believed that I was redeemable, I would have tried to persuade my husband to stay home and not immigrate to America. As I lay miserably alone in that hospital bed, I remember giving a desperate glance heavenward. It was all I could manage, but it was enough. I am a prayer, Lord, I said without words. Read me. Words are nice, but words are not needed when you are under the broom tree. Just be content to know that every word you would have said, if you could have said it, is heard loud and clear among the angels and by the Lord. His ears are especially tuned to those sorts of prayers – to the solitary, silent scream!

So where does this leave our hero? Sadder and wiser, certainly. Elijah came to terms with his fallen humanity. The expert on the subject of prayer learned that there are some times when you run out. You run out of faith, out of energy, out of friends, and out of hope. You run out of the human resources to function anymore. You run out of belief, and you run out of ideas, and you even run out of prayers. When that happens, God has only just begun! As Elijah was to find out, God gives more grace, more help, more joy, more hope, and more strength to all of us in our weakness than He ever does when we are strong. We just need to bank on it.

*Adapted from Prayer That Works By Jill Briscoe, ©2000, Used by permission of Tyndale House Publishers, Inc. Wheaton, Illinois. All rights reserved.*

# 6

# How to Hear God's Voice Above the Clamor

**How to incorporate contemplative prayer into your everyday life.**

## by Stacey Padrick-Thompson

God desires for us to be intimate with Him. And true intimacy requires more than just speaking to Him – it involves listening to Him as well. I used to think, *If only God would speak more clearly, I would follow Him more closely.* But at unexpected times, stopping from my jog to watch a sunset, or gazing at a starry evening sky, I have heard Him, the voice of a friend, a friend longing to be heard and waiting for my ears to be open and attentive.

God desires to communicate with His people, even more than we desire to communicate with Him! I have learned to hear His voice through listening prayer–what some call contemplative prayer. You may think of contemplative prayer as a practice only of saints and mystics in bygone eras. But it is not limited to a particular type of person, a particular era, nor is it reserved for the "super spiritual." Contemplative prayer is a form of prayer that all believers today can enjoy.

### WHAT IS CONTEMPLATIVE PRAYER?

So what exactly is contemplative prayer? How can we incorporate it into our busy daily lives? Contemplative prayer is thoughtful, reflective prayer. It requires effort. It demands active listening, focused attention, and confident expectation that God will speak.

In contemplative prayer, we are still before God, reflecting, anticipating, listening, and waiting on Him. Throughout the Psalms, David models one who waits on God in this way: "My soul waits in silence for God only" (Ps. 62:1, NASB). "My soul thirsts for God, for the living God. When can I go and meet with God?" (Ps. 42:2).

Contemplative prayer is being with God, empty-handed, waiting attentively for whatever He wants to speak, to show, or to do. Why is simply sitting at His feet with no agenda so difficult – even frightening?

Most of us argue that we haven't "enough time." Those of us who have taken time may complain that God doesn't seem to speak clearly. I recognize other reasons for my avoidance. I am afraid of what I might hear. When I quietly wait on God, the Holy Spirit often speaks penetrating words – words of conviction, words of love, or no words at all.

With *words of conviction*, God reveals actions or attitudes I need to confess to Him and sometimes others and directs me to seek reconciliation. Only by listening to the Spirit's conviction can I recognize my sin and hear Him direct me to seek forgiveness.

At other times as I listen, God has exposed attitudes of mine that dishonor Him. For instance, when I have been wrought with anxiety about a situation I face, He has revealed that my anxiety reflects a lack of trust in Him.

Surprisingly, I often find myself just as reluctant to hear His *words of love*–particularly when I feel less than lovable. Hearing His words of grace and love can be painfully difficult. Many of us don't wait in His presence long enough to let Him love us. We are quick to voice our concerns, seek His guidance, and request His blessing. Yet, how it must grieve our Father's heart that we come to Him only in want of something, rather than coming simply because we enjoy being in the Father's presence.

Perhaps another reason we hesitate to practice contemplative, listening prayer is we fear hearing no *words at all*. We strive to attain some tangible result validating the use of our time, even our devotional time with God. We become unable to enjoy the delight of simply being with Him. Yet, as two lovers are content to be in each other's presence, not needing always to speak, God delights for us to sit at His feet and enjoy being with Him.

## PUTTING IT INTO PRACTICE

How can we begin to practice contemplative prayer? The following are suggestions to explore.

### 1. Meditate on Scripture. *"I will meditate on your precepts" (Ps. 119:78).*

Choose one verse, phrase, or word upon which to meditate. Ponder it. Slowly repeat it. Ask the Lord what He wants to speak to you through it. Taste the richness of His spiritual food and its nourishment for your life.

### 2. Sing and pray the Psalms. *"Sing praise to the Lord!" (Ps. 68:32).*

After reading a psalm, begin to sing it to a tune you know or create as you go along. I find that singing a psalm helps me ponder it afresh.

Try praying a psalm as if you had written the words from your heart. During my stay at a monastery, I joined the monks as they chanted a few chapters of the Psalms each morning and evening.

### 3. Journal in prayer.

Write your prayers to God and wait for His response. Writing helps us stay focused and enables us to probe our thoughts and heart more deeply. Try an exercise called "Dialogue with God." Write something you want to tell God (for instance, a statement rather than a question). Asking the Holy Spirit to guide you, write what you sense is His response to your statement. Continue the dialogue until you believe God has finished speaking to you.

For example, while struggling with a chronic illness, I wrote in my journal:

*Stacey: Lord, I know You can heal me.*

*God: Yes, I can heal you, but I want to heal your spirit first. Will you let Me heal your spirit and wait on My timing to heal your body?*

When I first learned this exercise, I was very reluctant. How presumptuous to think I could write God's response to me! Yet, I beheld with amazement His words to me through this exercise – words very different from what I expected to hear. God also points out the enemy's lies I have been listening to and directs me to claim His words of truth. I recommend writing with a Bible nearby to refer to as He leads.

### 4. Take a walk in nature and listen to God speak to you through His creation.

"The heavens declare the glory of God; the skies proclaim the work of his hands. Day after day they pour forth speech; night after night they display knowledge" (Ps.19:1-2).

When I take time to thoughtfully observe God's creation, He tangibly teaches me His Word. While I sit alone on a beach, absorbed in the power and constancy of the waves, He reminds me that His love for me is constant.

### 5. Be still before Him.

"The LORD is good to those who wait for Him, to the person who seeks Him. It is good that he waits silently.... Let him sit alone and be silent" (Lam. 3:25-26,28, NASB). In this posture of stillness, we can more keenly hear Him speak. We honor God by expressing our willingness to be still in His presence.

We may find it difficult and uncomfortable at first to relinquish our needs-oriented approach to prayer. But I firmly believe we delight God's heart when we come to Him not to receive or give Him anything, but rather simply to delight ourselves in Him (Ps 37:4). Allow

Him to express His love and joy over you. If total stillness is difficult, try the following exercises. After closing your eyes and stilling your body, become aware of your breathing. As you slowly inhale, think on a name of Jesus:

- Meditate on this name as you slowly speak it to yourself, reflecting upon all that it means; for example: Bread of Life, Good Shepherd, Master, Light of the World, the Vine, the Door, the Resurrection and the Life, Alpha and Omega ...

- Or meditate on the names of God: Deliverer, Rock, Strong Tower, Jehovah-Jireh (Provider), Jehovah-Rapha (the Lord who Heals), I AM, Abba ...

- A similar exercise helps when I am anxious. I slowly inhale, saying to myself Jesus' name, and with each exhalation I release a fear or worry that is on my mind. Then, I continue to think on Jesus' name.

Try scheduling a longer period of time once a week for contemplation. Reflect on the events of the week, conversations, unexpected news, a sermon, or something you are reading. I like to see it as "making a date with God." Go for a walk alone with Him, or sit with a cup of coffee and talk to Him freely, listen, and enjoy being with Him.

Developing a discipline takes perseverance. Our flesh does not like to be trained and controlled. We will find every reason not to practice contemplative prayer. But as we sit with Him in faith and obedience, He will honor our desire to know and hear Him. Do not be discouraged if you do not hear anything. God often wants us to sit in stillness at His feet and learn to be content in His presence. Pray for the desire and grace to communicate with God in this intimate way.

# 7

# 20 Ways to Wake Up Your Quiet Time

**Creative, thoughtful ways for energizing your quiet time with God.**

### by Pam Farrel

Behind closed doors, many of us yawn through our quiet times. Somehow, our routine time with God slowly and quietly degenerates into a boring, predictable rut. As spiritual cataracts grow over our sleepy eyes, we may grow disinterested and frustrated. Such seasons demand a fresh view of the Creator. Like any good relationship, quiet times with God need a little variety. Instead of rolling over and hitting the snooze button, try one of these ideas for your next quiet time.

### 1. WRITE A LETTER TO GOD ABOUT YOUR LIFE.
Give it to a friend to email back to you in three months. In the letter, talk to God about the areas of your life that are bothering you. Write about how you'd like to grow and what attribute of His you'd like to see more clearly.

### 2. WRITE OUT AND PERSONALIZE SCRIPTURE BY INSERTING YOUR NAME INTO PROISES RELEVANT TO YOUR LIFE OR CURRENT STRUGGLES.
For example, I would personalize Psalm 84:11 in this way: "No good thing does God withhold from Pam when she walks uprightly." Many of the Bible's promises come to life and seem more powerful and relevant when personalized in this way. Spend some time meditating and praying over verses that you personalize. I once copied a set of verses and strung them together as a personalized love letter from God's heart to my own. I have it framed and hanging in my room. Those personalized verses help me keep a big view of God.

### 3. GO ON A PRAISE WALK.
Thank God for everything you see. Take the opportunity to look closely at God's creation, praising Him for His creativity and the beauty of the world He's crafted. After hiking for a while, find a quiet spot to read one of the many psalms that describe His creation. Isaiah 40 and

Genesis 1 are two other chapters that will help you focus your heart and mind on God's creative character.

### 4. READ THROUGH THE BIBLE, MARK IT UP, AND GIVE IT AS A GIFT TO A CHILD.

If you begin early, you can plan to give the Bible as a gift to your child before an important transition, such as when he or she enters high school, leaves home, enters college, or gets married. Try to picture God through his or her eyes. With that season of life in mind, mark verses you think will help your child see and trust God in the transition to come. You might also make notes in the margin to help guide and direct the child's thinking about a passage or explain how the passage is relevant to this stage of life.

### 5. SPEND YOUR ENTIRE TIME WITH GOD SINGING AND PRAISING HIM.

Church hymnals and books of choruses are great resources to enliven your quiet time with personal worship. You might even try creating a song of your own!

### 6. DANCE BEFORE THE LORD LIKE DAVID, WHO DANCED "WITH ALL HIS MIGHT" (2 SAM. 6:14).

David's dancing was a heartfelt and spontaneous expression of rejoicing. So put on your favorite hymn or praise song, and dance away. Interpretive dance is a wonderful way to express your heart and soul in praise before God. If you enjoy Jewish folk dancing, ballet, or some other kind of dance, dedicate your talent to God.

### 7. WRITE DOWN EVERY SIN THAT CONTINUES TO HAUNT YOU.

Then write 1 John 1:9 over each sin. Destroy the list – God has. This is a strong visual reminder of how God blots out your sin.

### 8. WRITE OUT A PHILIPPIANS 4:8 LIST.

What is lovely to you, worthy of praise, excellent, etc.? Hang the list in a place where you tend to be grumpy, such as above the washer and dryer or on the dashboard of your car for that frustrating commute!

### 9. PRAY IN A POSTURE YOU DON'T NORMALLY USE.

Try praying on your knees, prone, or standing with your face to the heavens and your hands raised in worship. It's amazing how simply changing your posture before God can change your attitude and help you experience Him in new ways.

### 10. READ A DIFFERENT TRANSLATION OF THE BIBLE.

You might consider purchasing a Bible that has several translations in parallel. Reading a new translation or comparing different ones can stimulate new insights into Scripture. If you've used and marked up one particular Bible for many years, reading a different Bible will enable you to see the Word with new vision. Because your eyes will not be drawn to notes and highlighted passages from previous study or devotional reading, the Scripture will feel as beautiful and inviting as a fresh snowfall on a crisp winter morn.

### 11. PRAISE JESUS FROM A TO Z.

For example, "Jesus, You are amazing...Jesus, You are beautiful..." This activity will challenge you to think deeply about who Jesus is and why you love and serve Him. As you praise Jesus using each letter of the alphabet, spend some time meditating on each word you use to describe Him. Thinking deeply about Him is more important than racing through each letter of the alphabet as fast as you can.

### 12. WRITE OUT YOUR PRAYERS TO JESUS.

You might write them in a journal, or purchase special stationery for these precious letters, as you might do if you were sending a letter to someone you have fallen deeply in love with. At the end of the letter, sign your name, just as you would a normal letter. Something powerful and deeply intimate happens when you record your thoughts and prayers in a letter to Jesus.

### 13. MAKE A LIST OF THE HURTS AND NEEDS IN YOUR LIFE.

As you come to a verse that shows how God can meet that need, write it down next to that need. Like the letters mentioned above, you can do this in your journal, or separately. You might even create a journal that records only your needs and relevant Scriptures. As you do this, you create your own book of God's promises!

### 14. REREAD THE NOTES OF THE SERMON FROM THE PREVIOUS WEEK.

If your pastor is doing a series and you know what Scriptures he'll be addressing next, read ahead in the passage to be covered next Sunday. This will prepare you to think more deeply and listen better during the next sermon, as well as helping you remember and apply truth. Find a verse in the text that has helped you grow, and write a note to your pastor thanking him for his sermon and insight on the passage.

### 15. READ YOUR FAVORITE HYMN.

Spend some time meditating about each of the hymn's verses and its overall message. Find the Bible passage that the hymn was based on, and think about how the hymn was composed. What were the circumstances? Your pastor or worship leader might know about a particular hymn's origin. Your Christian bookstore may also carry books that detail the history of certain hymns. If you're able to locate such information, think about how the hymn reflects the author's response to God during his or her circumstances.

### 16. SPEND A PERIOD OF TIME FASTING FROM FOOD, TV, OR A HOBBY TO SPEND MORE TIME WITH GOD.

If you're able, combine your fast with a day at a quiet retreat center, the beach, the mountains, or even tucked away in a library to reflect on God's Word and His hand in your life.

### 17. HAVE A QUIET TIME WITH ONE OF YOUR CHILDREN OR GRANDCHILDREN.

This would probably include reading a passage from the Bible out loud. You can give children a powerful peek into your relationship with Christ by inviting them to share your regular time with God. As you ask them questions about what they see in the passage, you'll teach them to think more deeply about God's Word. Their responses and observations may surprise you, stretch you, and enrich your own perspective.

### 18. WRITE ABOUT YOUR RELATIONSHIP WITH GOD FROM A DIFFERENT POINT OF VIEW.

Think about how someone else would describe your walk. For example, my teen son might say, "My mom has a radical walk with Jesus. She really got pegged (convicted) by this verse." Several friends from the mission field explained how this activity helped them communicate the parable of the sower to the tribe they worked with. In their translation work, they described the seed that grew as the one that fell on "mulchy" soil. In that tribe, the best heart is one that resembles a compost pile. When you consider your walk and God's Word from the perspective of another, you will think differently, cross cultural barriers, and gain a fresh view of God.

### 19. MEMORIZE ONE OF THE PRAYERS OF THE BIBLE, SUCH AS MARY'S PRAYER IN LUKE 1:46-55.

Then act the prayer out as a soliloquy.

### 20. WRITE OUT A LIST OF THEOLOGICAL QUESTIONS YOU'D LIKE ANSWERED.

Choose one and begin researching it. "God, what is Your heart toward women?" was a question I had that led me on an exhaustive study of all the women in the Bible, and all the verses with the words woman and women in them.

## ABIDING DAILY

Remember the purpose of all these ideas is to enhance your relationship with God and your intimacy with Him during your quiet time. The goal is to abide ever more in Him. As Fern Nichols, the founder of Moms in Touch, says, "If you seek to abide in the vine daily, you never know what day He might choose to change your life forever." Enjoy the adventure!

*This article was adapted from* Woman of Influence: Ten Traits of Those Who Want to Make a Difference *by Pam Farrel, ©1996 by Pam Farrel.*

# 8

# Rest for the Weary

**A missionary shares the importance of getting away from it all to renew your spirit – especially when you don't think you can afford the time.**

by Denele Ivins

My hands gripped the steering wheel as my mini-van cut through the ranch-strewn countryside of eastern Oregon. I was escaping to a retreat center for missionaries, in desperate need of rest and restoration. It had been nine months since we packed up our lives in East Asia and returned to the U.S. After 18 years of Asian life, our move back to the States was not a return "home," but a painful uprooting for our family.

As I drove, my mind raced with doubts and guilt: "I don't really need to do this. What kind of mother leaves her family for a week with an empty refrigerator? I should have brought them along; they need it too."

But as the miles passed, the rural landscape and the quietness began to work magic. I already felt calmer – and hope was building in me that God might use this time away to restore me.

Heading home five days later, my mind was still busy, but with thoughts of a different type. As I thought of my husband and children, I was able to pray for them in a deeper, more trusting way than I had for a long time. My heart for ministry, which had been numb, was waking up. I dreamed of taking a group from our church back to our adopted land on a short-term missions trip. I broke the nine-month musical silence and sang praise songs in my van. All at once, as I maneuvered curving mountain roads, I realized that I was refreshed. Creativity and energy and praise were returning – and hope had been restored.

## THE ROAD TO RECOVERY

My five days at a retreat center was just what I needed. But how did I even know that I needed to get away? And in all my numbness and weariness, how did I ever manage the energy and commitment it takes for a mother of three to escape?

I'd love to say that it was my wisdom that made me schedule my three recent personal retreats. The truth is that I was weary to my core and unable to take any action to help myself. Caring brothers and sisters saw my condition and made a diagnosis: emotional exhaustion and possible burnout because of the trauma of our transition back to life in the U.S. Beyond a diagnosis, God was gracious to give them a care plan to restore me back to emotional health.

Our home church and sending organization do a fantastic job of caring for their overseas staff–and in my need I was the recipient of this care. Our home church sent us to Colorado to attend a week of debriefing and renewal for missionaries in transition. Through this time, I began to understand how very tired I was. I left China tired, and then, as moms do, I set aside my need for rest to attend to the huge task of settling my children–grades 6, 8, and 12–into their new lives in their passport country. Our sending organization very gently but persistently suggested the value of taking a sabbatical after 18 years of serving overseas. My husband was able to take a manner of one, but I found myself unable to even sit and read anything for more than five minutes.

My care counselor, Shirley Wilson, asked me about taking a sabbatical. My question, in a choked voice, was how could I when I faced the task of guiding my children through their transition. I can't just take off three months from life, I said.

"Why don't you take mini-sabbaticals?" Shirley asked. With some well-placed questions, she guided me to discover what would best refresh me. My deepest longing, she helped me see, was to get away by myself, in places with heavy doses of mountains and pine trees and quietness, where I could rest, explore, hike, bike, read, and pray.

### REST FOR MY SOUL

My first foray into solitude came seven weeks later. I wanted to quiet myself enough to hear God's voice. I took my Bible down to the creekside bench at the inn. My weariness was so deep that all I could do was open it up to the Psalms. I remember how I read a few verses, only to have my eyes blur over with tears. During my three days there, I did my part by showing up on that swing with God's Word in my lap, asking Him to restore me. And He did! One of the greatest burdens I carried with me on that first retreat was the deep disappointment for my daughter Claire and her college admissions process that year. A top student, Claire nonetheless was finding one door after another closing to her, leaving just one door open at the local university. My quiet time on that swing allowed me the chance to pour out my frustrations to God. Later, as I dozed next to the stream, His gentle voice spoke to me – "Claire needs roots." I was able to walk away from that three-day retreat with thankfulness for the scholarships to the local university–and feel a huge burden lifted.

## A MIRROR FOR REFLECTION

On my Oregon "mini-sabbatical," God revealed to me that the root reason for my weariness came mainly from the accumulation of the sacrifices of 18 years of living and reaching out cross-culturally.

One day I sat in the sunshine on my private deck, meditating on Psalm 20:1-3: "May the Lord answer you when you are in distress; may the name of the God of Jacob protect you. May he send you help from the sanctuary and grant you support from Zion. May he remember all your sacrifices and accept your burnt offerings."

I began by asking God to do these things for me. I could see how He had been doing them all along! He remembered my sacrifices even before I did–and I began recounting in my journal a long list of ways He had answered, protected, helped, and supported me.

## NURTURE FROM NATURE

Significant as these spiritual moments were for me, it would be dishonest to make it sound like I spent entire days in monk-like meditation. In truth, these deeper moments punctuated days full of walks, bike rides, hikes, meals out, and a good novel.

On my first trip, my walks were leisurely–mostly on the way to the small-town diner where I ate comfort food three times a day. But the springtime greenness and brilliant blue skies helped me rediscover both the beauty of my home state Idaho and the value of quietness. I cruised my van slowly down the country roads, marveling at the landscape carved out by the Snake River. On one drive down in the canyon, a bird burst into song just as I drove past; the beauty of it and a sense of God's love brought tears to my eyes.

This was physical restoration, after almost two decades of urban life –where instead of mountains, construction cranes rose above the horizon at every turn, and instead of the serenade of songbirds, the blare of taxi horns and yells of teeming life were what assaulted my senses.

The healing power of nature was just as important in my second and third retreats, but I felt more energetic and was able to be much more active, riding more than 50 miles of bike paths.

## CALLING ALL WOMEN!

Shirley's prescription for personal retreats was just what I needed to renew my body, mind, and soul. What has startled me is the reaction I get from other women when I tell them sheepishly about my mini-sabbatical events. I have read in their eyes everything from longing to outright jealousy. Women today are in desperate need of time away from their ministry and family responsibilities. The women's ministry pastor at my church said she feels guilty taking time away when there's so much to do. But just hearing my story has encouraged her to place a higher value on renewal—because, after all, it strengthens her for the tasks at hand.

## RESOLVED TO REST

As I climbed into the small back-country plane to leave my last retreat—feeling energetic, rested, and hopeful—I resolved not to wait until my weariness calls for emergency measures. I am determined to make this a lifelong habit—to take time out to seek solitude, rest, and renewal. To come to Him and let Him give me rest. Matthew 11:28-29 says, "Come to me, all you who are weary and burdened, and I will give you rest…. You will find rest for your souls."

# 9

# Soul Care

**Questions to ask yourself when assessing the state of your soul in the whirlwind of your busy life.**

by Linda Kline

If we're not careful, life can quickly empty our souls because we're constantly giving out. To give and give without being regularly replenished is to eventually become barren and dry. This is a battle we must continually fight. The ache in our hearts that won't go away is our souls crying out for attention. That's why it's so important that we stop and find Jesus in the midst of the demands of life. Our souls need to be cared for. There is precious counsel and comfort that comes from intimacy with the Father. Caring for our souls is the only way to not find ourselves empty or just surviving. We must do whatever it takes to maintain the wellness of our souls.

The concept of our soul (*nepesh* in Hebrew, *psuche* in Greek) refers to the self, life, breath, the heart, the very essence of a person. The soul is the very core of who God created us to be. To care for my soul means that I draw on God at all levels–mentally, emotionally, relationally, physically, and spiritually–and that I am being consistently transformed, renewed, and freed through the life of Jesus. It means to incorporate healthy rhythms into my life so that I am able to truly be myself and pour into others out of a full tank. "Only give heed to yourself and keep your soul diligently" (Deut. 4:9, NASB).

Our model in this (and hopefully in every aspect of life) is Jesus. Henri Nouwen's classic article "Moving from Solitude to Community to Ministry" is so helpful in learning to feed your soul. We see patterns of Jesus pulling away from the crowds to be alone with the Father, drawing life from unhurried, uninterrupted intimacy. We see Him interacting in authentic community, gathering around the table, sharing day-to-day life with friends and family. We see Him pouring out His power in the ministry, taking His marching orders from His Father instead of being pulled in every direction by the manipulation and control of others.

It's so easy to lose yourself in ministry life. Instead of Jesus' healthy, holy rhythms of solitude, community, and ministry, we run on a cycle of "Run, Crash, Burn, Recover, and Repeat." For many of us, our soul runs on fumes. Instead of being well-tended and well-fed, our soul shrivels from benign neglect, leaving us tired, weary, and apathetic at best…bitter, angry, and resentful at worst.

Here are a few questions.

## SOLITUDE

Our twenty-first century life of busyness, noise, social media, and technology leads to what consultant Linda Stone calls "Continuous Partial Attention" or CPA. We become incapable of giving our full attention to our spouse, our children, our friends, our work, and especially to God. We were not designed to remain "always on," hyper-connected 24/7/365. "And He said to them, 'Come away by yourselves to a secluded place and rest a while'" (Mark 6:31-32, NASB).

- Do I know how to enjoy being alone with God? (For many, the thought of solitude is equated with loneliness instead of joyful, refueling connection with Jesus.)
- Is there enough silence and stillness in my life to hear the voice of God through the noise?
- Is there space in my life for God to act?
- Am I a "self-feeder"? Do I systematically study the Word, pray, and spend time with God on my own?
- Should I set aside a block of time—an afternoon, a day, a weekend—to just be with the Lord?
- Is my life too busy, too loud, too scheduled, or too "peopled"?
- Am I afraid of being alone with God?
- Do I know how to sit in solitude at Jesus' feet?

## COMMUNITY

God designs us to connect on a vertical plane with Him and on a horizontal plane with others. "Let him who cannot be alone beware of community. Let him who is not in community beware of being alone. Each by itself has profound pitfalls and perils. One who wants fellowship without solitude plunges into the void of words and feelings, and one who seeks solitude without fellowship perishes in the abyss of vanity, self-infatuation, and despair" (Dietrich Bonhoeffer, *Life Together*, 78).

- Do I have true friendships? Or just acquaintances? Sadly, most people in ministry have few or no genuinely life-giving friends.

- Is my spouse one of my best friends?
- Has ministry taken a toll on my marriage? My family?
- Do I have any spiritually-deep connections? Do I have any soul friends?
- Am I trying to be a "Lone Ranger" Christian?
- Are there people in my life who know and love God and know and love me enough to give me the hug and slug I need? Do I have the needed accountability to warn me when I'm heading in the wrong direction?
- Which friends provide mutual, reciprocal support and encouragement?
- Who in my life consistently points me toward Jesus?
- When did I last laugh until my face hurt? How do I have fun? Do I play? Do I have anyone to play with?

## MINISTRY

I truly want to be able to say, as Jesus did: "I glorified You on the earth, having accomplished the work which You have given Me to do" (John17:4, NASB). But there is so much work to do. I get sidetracked by the demands and I feel inadequate to the task. Soul care ensures that my ministry flows from the Lord, not from my own limited strength.

- Am I taking in without giving out or am I giving out without taking in?
- Does my ministry flow out of my communion with God and my connections in the body of Christ?
- Am I serving out of gratitude, love, obedience, and freedom?
- Is there a root of self, guilt, performance, pride, competition?
- Am I coming to God with my availability alone for His plans— rather than my own agenda?
- It may be very challenging, but is there joy in ministry?
- Am I working out of my spiritual gifts? Do I know what my spiritual gifts are?
- Am I doing what God has assigned? Or do I run myself ragged trying to meet the expectations of others as well as my own?

A well-tended soul is alive toward God, enjoys true community with others, and is comfortable in her own skin. We must be proactive stewards to honestly say, "It is well with my soul."

# 10

# Food for the Soul

**The many benefits of spending regular alone time with God.**

### by Jean Fleming

A young German woman told me that when she came to this country, she was offended when she was referred to as an alien. Until then she had only heard the term used to describe someone from outer space!

If you are a true believer in Jesus Christ, the Bible calls you an alien. Peter says believers are "aliens and strangers" in the world (1 Peter 2:11, NASB). When you became a child of God, you began to live between two worlds–this one on earth and your eternal home in heaven. Jesus said that you are no longer of this world any more than He is (John 17:14-16). But while you live here physically, God tells you to fix your eyes on the real but invisible life you have with Christ.

How do we as aliens keep our attention on the spiritual realms–the unseen things above–when the seen world is glittering around us? How do we as strangers and pilgrims maneuver on earth while keeping our eyes on heaven? To navigate this challenging terrain, we need to fix our eyes on the truths of God every day.

Quiet time is a place where we can fix our eyes on God and the invisible realities of our lives. Take a look at just some of the many benefits of spending regular time alone with God.

## A PLACE TO RENEW

God calls you to live by faith. This means believing and acting with confidence based on unseen realities (Heb. 11:1). All the while, the visible, tangible world exerts its gravitational pull. You don't intend it, but the compass of your soul is pulled off true north. The Bible strongly warns and urges you:

> *Do not conform any longer to the pattern of this world, but be transformed by the renewing of your mind. Then you will be able to test and approve what God's will is–his good, pleasing and perfect will.* – Rom. 12:2

God calls you to preside over the care of your soul so that it is not squeezed into the world's mold. He wants you to actively engage in re-shaping your mind according to His truth. Quiet time helps you renew your mind. Then you can live by faith, not by sight.

## A PLACE TO KNOW YOURSELF

Living between two worlds can create an identity crisis. Who will tell you who you are? If you define who you are based on the feedback you receive from the world, you will be accepting misinformation. Don't look to others to assign value to you, to tell you how you fit into the scheme of things. They can't. Only the God who created and redeemed you can tell you who you are, why you're here, and where you're going.

In the movie *My Fair Lady*, Eliza Doolittle is transformed from a poor cockney flower girl into a glamorous, cultured woman. Many books and movies are based on the idea that there is a prince inside our froggy selves. One of the reasons we respond to that idea is because it is rooted in truth. The Bible teaches that you are a new creation in Christ (2 Cor. 5:17). But your new self doesn't emerge by singing "The Rain in Spain" or burst forth after a prince's kiss.

This is why quiet time is so important. God is the only one who can tell you who you are because He designed you in the womb and He gave you second birth in Jesus Christ. Just as physical birth is merely the beginning, so spiritual birth is a starting point from which to grow, learn, and develop. In Christ you have a new identity. The trouble is that as you scuff along here on earth, you easily forget that God has chosen you and changed you (John 15:16, Eph. 1:4) and that you are a citizen of heaven (Phil. 3:20).

## A PLACE TO REMEMBER

You need to be reminded every day that God loves you (Eph. 2:4), that His plans for you are good (Jer. 29:11), and that He will never leave you or forsake you (Heb. 13:5). Consider His death in your place and His desire for you to live with Him in heaven forever–and marvel.

> *The LORD your God is with you, he is mighty to save. He will take great delight in you, he will quiet you with his love, he will rejoice over you with singing.*
> – Zeph. 3:17

## A PLACE TO BE WHOLE

You were created for fellowship with God. The words salvation and blessing, which pop up everywhere in the Bible, burst with the promise of good coming to you because you belong to Jesus Christ. You were created for a wholeness that you cannot know apart from relationship with God. David expressed it this way: "You make known to me the path of life; you will fill me with joy in your presence, with eternal pleasures at your right hand" (Ps. 16:11).

## A PLACE TO KNOW GOD

When Jesus Christ appeared to Paul on the road to Damascus, Paul asked, "Who are You, Lord" (Acts 9:5)? What a great question–a question that only God can answer. Because God is invisible, eternal, infinite, and holy, we are dependent on His revelation of Himself. Our notion of God must be shaped by what He says about Himself, or else we create a god in our own minds that is as much an idol as one carved from wood or stone. A.W. Tozer wrote:

*It is impossible to keep our moral practices sound and our inward attitudes right while our idea of God is erroneous or inadequate. If we would bring back spiritual power to our lives, we must begin to think of God more nearly as He is.*

## A PLACE TO CHANGE

Quiet time reminds you that God intends for you to become like Christ (Rom. 8:29). It is not only possible for you to be changed; it is imperative. In fact, if you are not different since your "conversion," perhaps you have not yet come to true faith in Jesus Christ. Woven into the warp and woof of life in Christ is the assumption of change. A changed life is the validation of your encounter with God. This change doesn't happen all at once or without accompanying failures. But authentic change is inherent in our life with Christ.

Change takes place as we focus our attention on Christ and reflect His likeness.

*And we, who with unveiled faces all reflect the Lord's glory, are being transformed into his likeness with ever-increasing glory, which comes from the Lord, who is the Spirit.*
– 2 Cor. 3:18

Twelfth-century monk Bernard of Clairvaux comments on this idea: "His features we see not; and yet they mold us, not by their outward beauty striking on our bodily sight, but by the love and joy they kindle in our hearts."

## A PLACE TO BE FED

Time with the Lord is soul food, necessary for the life and satisfaction of your soul. Books with the word soul in the title have been hot sellers recently. People sense a hunger for something that can touch their essence. But unless a book on the care of the soul calls the reader to come to Jesus and His Word, it cannot keep its promise. The prophet Isaiah records God's warning and invitation:

*Why spend money on what is not bread, and your labor on what*

*does not satisfy? Listen, listen to me, and eat what is good, and*
*your soul will delight in the richest of fare. Give ear and come to*
*me; hear me, that your soul may live. I will make an everlasting*
*covenant with you, my faithful love promised to David.*
– Is. 55:2-3

A tasty, attractively presented meal shared with friends is one of life's true pleasures. A good meal in good company is a taste of what God wants for your soul. Quiet time is fellowship with God over the delicious and nourishing fare of His Word. When the Lord says, "'Your soul will delight in the richest of fare," He tells you to come to Him and listen to Him. You need to hear God's words spoken to you if you are to experience joy in your deepest places. No wonder Jeremiah said, "When your words came, I ate them; they were my joy and my heart's delight" (Jer. 15:16). Remember, man does not live on bread alone.

## A PLACE TO REFOCUS

Quiet time can keep you from frittering your life away on the extraneous, the peripheral. In a culture that exalts and feeds busyness, quiet time can refocus your attention daily on what really matters. God will remind you that your relationship with Him is supreme; everything else must be subordinate to that relationship. When you pause in God's presence, the fog clears and values sharpen. You realign yourself with the commitments you've made to God and others. The important things emerge, and the secondary things recede once again. The busier you are, the more desperately you need the pause that refreshes.

## A PLACE TO HEAL

Humans have been called the "walking wounded." All of us take a battering from time to time and need the healing touch of our Lord. In times of pain, confusion, and anguish, King David knew to retreat into God's presence. In 2 Samuel 12, God sent word that David's young son, who was conceived in an adulterous relationship with Bathsheba, was going to die. David, in great agony of spirit, fasted and prayed. He laid on the floor for seven days and prayed that God might spare the child. But when this son died, everyone noticed something strange. David got up off the floor, washed, changed his clothes, worshiped God, ate, and comforted his wife.

Those who observed this were astonished. They asked, "Why are you acting this way? While the child was alive, you fasted and wept, but now that the child is dead, you get up and eat!"

The explanation lies with God's healing power. When David secluded himself in God's presence, he received forgiveness for his sin. He gained an eternal perspective regarding his son's death. He was fortified in his faith so that he was able to trust God in a painful loss. He experienced the grace of God and the balm of God's comfort and strength, so he could offer solace to his grieving wife.

I have friends whose daughter took her own life, friends whose son was murdered, friends who experienced sexual abuse, friends whose teenaged son died of cancer. Excruciating pain won't yield to easy answers or clichés. For my friends, the ongoing process of healing began and continues in God's presence.

## A PLACE FOR QUESTIONS

Bill had questions. Lots of them. Over years of enduring a long and painful illness, Bill prayed, "Lord, what do You want me to learn from this? What is the purpose of pain? How do You want me to respond?" Bill asked his pastor and friends for their insights. But most of all, Bill asked God his questions. At Bill's memorial service, several people mentioned his pattern of asking and seeking in the midst of his pain.

In quiet time, you can ask your questions. God intends for the circumstances of your life to lead you into deeper interaction with Him. He wants your questions and struggles to drive you in His direction. What are you facing? What questions do you have about life? Pray, "Open my eyes that I may see wonderful things in your law" (Ps. 119:18). He delights in answering this prayer. Once you ask, lean toward God in anticipation. Read the Bible in His presence, and listen to what His Spirit might say to you.

Your questions may surface from your Bible reading. "What does it mean 'to abide'?" "How do I grow in grace?" Jesus promised,

> *Ask and it will be given to you; seek and you will find; knock and the door will be opened to you. For everyone who asks receives; he who seeks finds; and to him who knocks, the door will be opened.*
> – Matt. 7:7-8

Spiritual truth is revealed to those who seek it. Asking, seeking, and knocking imply time, effort, and persistence.

Make your quiet time a place where you withdraw with God to ask your questions about life and His teachings. Ask. Seek. Knock. And then hang around to listen. The answers may not come all at once. It pleases God that you are turning to Him asking Him to help you make sense of life.

## A PLACE FOR CONFIDENCE

The marriage vow has never guaranteed happiness or durability. Many forfeit the promise of faithfulness to their partner. Business contracts are annulled in legal high stepping. Mothers and fathers deny natural affection for their children and neglect and abuse those given to their care. The world is a precarious and unsure place. If you put your confidence in people, social structures, or the legal system, you find that the footing invariably gives way. Even if you are blessed with honorable and godly human relationships, you may outlive them. Nothing and no one can promise to be there for you always. God is the only one who can keep that promise.

## STAYING FOCUSED

The benefits of quiet time are more numerous than can be mentioned here. Quiet time helps spiritual aliens keep their gaze sharply focused on Christ and His kingdom so that they may live between two worlds, serving the kingdom of God on earth. These pilgrims need continual intense contact with their true, though unseen, life. Greatest delight is found in consistent meetings with God. This is, after all, what we aliens were made for.

# ~ Author Biographies ~

**Jane Rubietta** a is an award-winning author of 13 books. Her newest book is *Finding the Messiah*, a 29-day Advent reader. Additionally, she speaks internationally, ministering to women. Jane and her husband live in Park Ridge, Illinois. Visit her at JaneRubietta.com to learn more about her books and speaking ministry.

**Shelly Esser** has been the editor of *Just Between Us*, a magazine encouraging and equipping women for a life of faith, for the last 25 years. She has written numerous articles and a book, and ministered to women for over 25 years. She and her husband live in southeastern Wisconsin. They have four daughters and a son-in-law.

**Jill Briscoe** is a popular writer and conference speaker who has authored over 50 books and travels all over the world. Jill is executive editor of *Just Between Us*, a magazine encouraging and equipping women for a life of faith. Jill and her husband, Stuart, have been in ministry for over 50 years and have a worldwide radio ministry, *Telling the Truth*. She and her husband live in suburban Milwaukee, Wisconsin, have three grown children, and thirteen grandchildren.

**Stacey Padrick-Thompson** is the author of *Living with Mystery: Finding God in the Midst of Unanswered Questions*. She holds a degree in Spiritual Direction and serves in many roles at her church including leading the liturgy, worship, and teaching Sunday school. She is currently working on a devotional and blog for moms seeking to spiritually thrive on the parenting journey. She lives in Novato, California.

**Pam Farrel**, along with her husband Bill, has worked in ministry for over 35 years. She is a relationship expert founding the marriage ministry Love-Wise, with her husband. Pam has written over 40 books, including the *10 Best Decisions* series, which have been translated into more than 14 languages. She has three sons and three daughters-in-law, as well as four grandchildren. Pam lives in San Diego, California. Contact her at www.Love-Wise.com.

**Denele Ivins** is an editor and serves in a global ministry, with her husband. They live in Boise, Idaho.

**Linda Kline** is Pastoral Director of Psalm One, a ministry of Bible teaching, Christ-centered spiritual formation, and soul care around the U.S. and overseas. Linda lives in Mason, Ohio.

**Jean Fleming** and her husband have served with The Navigators for nearly 50 years. Additionally, she is the author of *A Mother's Heart, Feeding Your Soul,* and *Pursue the Intentional Life* (all NavPress). Jean and her husband have three married children and nine grandchildren. They live in Montrose, Colorado.